My Hope

Poems by Eugene L. Clark

A
BACK TO THE BIBLE
PUBLICATION

Back to the Bible
Lincoln, Nebraska 68501

70,000 printed to date—1979
(5-6753—70M—19)
ISBN 0-8474-1213-X

Printed in the United States of America

Contents

Pages 9, 131 by Harold M. Lambert; pages 25, 73, 87 by Harry
Broman; pages 35, 67, 99, 105, 111, 125, 133 by Bill Myers;
page 79 by Camerique; page 117 by Nebraska Game Commission.

Comfort and Peace

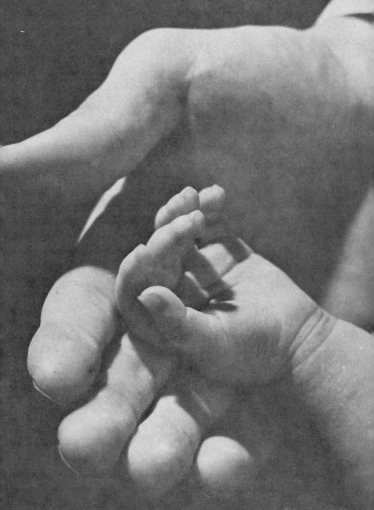

My Hope

Jesus is coming! It could be today,
It could be tomorrow, but surely one day.
The hope of His coming is blessed to me,
I long for the day when His face I shall see.

When weary with things that perplex and annoy,
And many things threaten my peace to destroy;
I think of His coming and soon they depart,
And peace once again reigns supreme in my heart.

I read of the mansions in heaven so fair,
And ponder the place He has gone to prepare;
And hope fills my soul as I go on my way,
Rejoicing to know that He may come today.

My hope for tomorrow sustains me today.
His Word like a lamp gives a light on my way.
I know that the future is in His control,
This hope for tomorrow brings peace to my soul.

Rest

When darkness, like an ocean wave, engulfs
   my soul,
When pitfalls, dangerous in light, are hidden now,
It is then that I rejoice in knowing it is true
That light and darkness are alike with Him,
   somehow.
Sometimes I pray, and light dissolves the darkness,
But sometimes darkness still remains, and I must
   trust
That He who knows no darkness sees the way
   before,
And in His love and wisdom will not be unjust.
Sometimes the light alone will burn and painful be.
Our toil and labor makes us weary in the day.
There is a rest that comes when quiet darkness
   falls,
And we by faith commit to Him our unseen way.

Jesus' Love Will Never Fail Me

Jesus' love will never fail me;
   He's a faithful friend and guide,
Leading me through joy and sorrow,
   Constantly He's by my side.

Jesus' love will never fail me.
   "Trust me," I can hear Him say,
"I will never, ever leave you,
   Nor forsake you, come what may."

Jesus' love will never fail me;
　His own life He freely gave,
Proving just how much He loved me,
　When He died my soul to save.

Jesus' love will never fail me;
　Faith and trust are on the throne;
Doubt and fear no longer haunt me,
　As I face things yet unknown.

Life will bring both joy and sorrow,
　On Jesus' love I can rely;
All things for my good are working,
　There's no need to question why.

Sunshine and Rain

The days were filled with sunshine,
The cloudless skies were blue;
The weather seemed so perfect,
No sign of rain in view.
But then I looked around me,
And all was desert sand;
The earth was parched and arid,
A dry and worthless land.

If life had only sunshine,
No stormy days or rain;
If everything were perfect,
No struggles and no pain;
It soon would be a desert.
So let us not complain;
The hard things make us stronger,
And growth comes with the rain.

Peace Is Only a Prayer Away

Why is your heart filled with worry and care?
Peace may be yours in a moment of prayer.
Lift up your heart as you need Him each day.
Peace is only a prayer away.

Life has its problems, its troubles and fears.
Sometimes its sorrows may bring us to tears;
Jesus is waiting to help you each day.
Peace is only a prayer away.

Why are you needlessly near to despair?
Jesus has promised your burden to bear.
Turn to Him now without further delay.
Peace is only a prayer away.

Is there a soul deeply troubled within,
Seeking for peace, overcome by your sin?
Victory is yours as you trust Him today.
Peace is only a prayer away.

Is He not able to meet every need?
Can He not do what He's promised indeed?
Fret not yourself or be filled with dismay.
Peace is only a prayer away.

Why does tomorrow bring fear to your heart?
Peace and contentment are His to impart.
Leave it with Him, He will show you the way.
Peace is only a prayer away.

Peace is only a prayer away.
Why longer wait, why further delay?
Your fears and tears He'll banish today.
His peace is only a prayer away.

In the Shadow of God's Hand

Suggested by Dr. George Sweeting

To the child of God who's walking
Close beside Him in the way,
Who is trusting Him completely
And obeying Him each day,
Like a shadow from His hand,
There's a place of sweet release;
In the midst of tribulation
There is rest and perfect peace.

There are shadows all around us
As we move along life's way,
Cast by fears and disappointments,
Bringing times of deep dismay;
But the shadow of God's hand
Is not ever far away,
When I step into its confines,
There is peace throughout the day.

When the heat of tribulation
Causes weariness of soul,
When in weakness I would stumble
As I cross some rocky knoll;
Then the shadow of God's hand
Brings release from anxious care,
And my fainting soul is strengthened
As we fellowship in prayer.

In the shadow of God's hand
There is freedom from all fear,
For the shadow's my assurance
That His hand is very near.

Angels

Do angels really gather 'round
When I have some great need?
This is the message that I get,
When I my Bible read.
I do not know just when and where
These angels work for me;
But I am glad to know they're there,
Although I cannot see.
This is another mystery
I do not understand,
But someday I will fully know
These wonders He has planned.

A Sense of Peace

When passing through the heat and fire,
Three things sustain my mind and heart;
Though still I may not understand,
A sense of peace they do impart.

Beyond all else, I must believe
That what my Father up above
Allows to come into my life
Is based on His unchanging love.

Then this, too, I must remember,
That nothing e'er escapes God's eye.
He is aware of everything.
He even knows before I cry.

And then this, too, I must believe
Down deep within my troubled soul,
That nothing in this universe
Is ever out of God's control.

As the Eagle

As the eagle cares for her own,
So God will care for me;
He never will neglect His own,
A faithful God is He.

Sometimes within the downy nest,
In comfort we are fed;
Sometimes with creature comforts gone,
In thorny ways we are led.

As the eagle's eye can see afar,
Where death and danger lie;
So God can see what lies ahead
And guide us with His eye.

With her own self, the mother bird
Protects her helpless young;
So Jesus gave Himself for us
And on a cross was hung.

With mighty wings the eagle lifts
Itself into the sky;
So wings of faith will lift us up
To a glorious home on high.

Ideas taken from a chapel sermon by Rev. Robert S. Peterson

Good News

There is good news for the lonely,
    You who are looking for love;
Seek not for comfort around you,
    Look to the Father above.

There is good news for the weary;
    "Come unto Me and find rest."
This is the promise of Jesus;
    Come and be one of the blessed.

There is good news for the sinner,
    There is redemption for all;
There is forgiveness in Jesus,
    Ask and He'll answer your call.

"Him that cometh to Me,
    I will in no wise cast out."
This is the promise He gives in His Word;
    Speak forth the message 'til all men have heard!

I Shall Not Want

In poverty I wandered,
    A sheep outside the fold,
Until the shepherd found me
    And brought me wealth untold.

In want I sought for something
    To satisfy my soul,
Until the shepherd found me,
    Restored and made me whole.

I thirsted for some water,
   My soul to satisfy.
He showed me springs of water
   That never would run dry.

In hunger I was searching
   Through deserts dry and bare,
Until the shepherd showed me
   His pasture green and fair.

I shall not want, for Jesus is my shepherd.
   He leadeth me beside the waters still.
In pastures green, He gently makes me down to lie.
   I shall not want, for He my soul shall fill.

Keep on Walkin', Pilgrim

Don't be weary, Pilgrim,
While trav'ling here below;
For there's a home awaiting,
The Bible tells me so.

Don't be hungry, Pilgrim,
Just bring your empty bowl;
There's manna in the Bible
To satisfy your soul.

Don't be thirsty, Pilgrim,
Just bring your cup to Him;
And God the Holy Spirit
Will fill it to the brim.

Don't be silent, Pilgrim,
While waiting for your King;
Let praises rise to meet Him,
Lift up your voice and sing.

Keep on walking, faithful Pilgrim.
The journey's leading home.

One Day at a Time

Forever is a long, long time;
    Eternity is mine.
I cannot comprehend it all,
    Just one day at a time.

If I could see beyond today,
    How anxious I would be;
The heartaches and the cares today
    Are quite enough for me.

My Father measures out each day
    With pleasure, pain and woe
That I may learn to trust His grace
    And in His likeness grow.

God graciously sends one day at a time;
    This is God's perfect design.
So why should I borrow the cares of tomorrow?
    He lovingly sends me one day at a time.

Take It to Jesus in Prayer

When the burdens of life seem too heavy to bear,
Why not take it to Jesus in prayer?
He has asked you to lay on Him each earthly care,
So take it to Jesus in prayer.

When the way seems so rough you can hardly
    move on,
Why not take it to Jesus in prayer?
When you're bowed down with trouble and hope
    seems all gone,
Just take it to Jesus in prayer.

When you're tempted to sin and your strength
    seems to fail,
Why not take it to Jesus in prayer?
No temptation's so great that we cannot prevail,
So take it to Jesus in prayer.

Oh, cast all your burdens on Jesus;
Go to the Saviour in prayer.
He promised to hear your petition;
Oh, take it to Jesus in prayer.

Peace Through Prayer
Philippians 4:6,7; John 14:27; Isaiah 26:3

Do not be anxious for anything,
    But let your requests be made known unto God;
And the peace that passeth all understanding
    Shall keep your heart and your mind.

Do not be troubled or be afraid,
    For Jesus has promised to give you His peace.
Perfect peace He offers to those who trust Him
    And seek Him often in prayer.

Go to the Saviour, O troubled soul!
    His peace He has promised to all who believe.
His Word, believing, by faith receiving;
    The peace of God will be yours.

I Believe That Jesus Loves Me

I believe that Jesus loves me,
    Though some things I can't explain;
Still I know His love surrounds me,
    Both in pleasure and in pain.

I believe that Jesus loves me,
    Once I feared the great unknown;
Now I trust His love completely;
    Faith sits calmly on the throne.

I believe that Jesus loves me;
    I can trust Him all the way.
"Child, I gave My life to save you,"
    I can hear Him softly say.

I believe that Jesus loves me,
    Come the darkness or the light;
On the mountain, through the valley,
    Trusting Him is my delight.

Joy or sorrow, pain or pleasure,
    Still He loves me, this I know;
He is working out His purpose,
    God's own Word has told me so.

Turn to the Bible

Perhaps you have sought satisfaction,
But somehow it never has come.
The questions of life go unanswered;
Your prospects have failed one by one.
But life still may bring you fulfillment:
Just open your Bible and read
From the source of all wisdom and knowledge;
God's Word is the guidebook you need.
Turn to the Bible, the answer is there.
Hope fills its pages, no need to despair.
There find the secret of peace for your soul.
Life will have meaning, a purpose, a goal.

When the world you had sought had been
    conquered,
When honor and praise came your way,
When success and acclaim were your portion,
When pleasure was king for a day,
You had no concern for the future.
And now these are passing away.
Your life that was full is now empty,
The glitter and gold turned to clay.
Turn to the Bible, the answer is there.
Hope fills its pages, no need to despair.
There find the secret of peace for your soul.
Life will have meaning, a purpose, a goal.

God's Changeless Love

Though every single flower dies,
And should the sun forget to rise
And every star fall from the skies,
Still, God's love for me would never change.

Though mother love should change to hate
And every man forsake his mate,
If every saint turned reprobate,
Still, God's love for me would never change.

Though every diamond turn to dust
And gold change into worthless rust,
If wrong should overcome the just,
Still, God's love for me would never change.

Though all the stars should cease to shine
Or fail to form their set design,
If all the wealth on earth were mine,
Still, God's love for me would never change.

Though every craftsman lost his skill
And all the songbirds became still,
If streams should turn and flow uphill,
Still, God's love for me would never change.

Though rocks should turn to crumbling clay
And night neglect to follow day,
If planets somehow lost their way,
Still, God's love for me would never change.

God's love for me will never, never change,
Though sun and moon and stars should fail to shine.
Though earth and heaven crumble into dust,
God's great, eternal, changeless, timeless love
will still be mine.

Witnessing
and
Service

A Spokesman

The silent stars away up high,
The sun and moon that rule the sky,
The drifting clouds and birds that fly
All speak of Thee.
Majestic mountains standing there,
The lily in the field so fair,
The flowers' fragrance in the air
All speak of Thee.
God's handiwork seen everywhere,
The unseen wind that stirs the air,
The instincts living creatures share
All speak of Thee.

Let nature speak!
Her wordless praises rise to Thee
Of all Thy wisdom, power and majesty,
Nor has she tongue or words to tell of Thee.
Make me a spokesman, Lord, I pray!
Use Thou my tongue
And grant me words to speak
Of Thy great grace,
Until salvation's plan and Calvary's love
Are clearly known to every man.

An Instrument

Lord, help me look at those I meet
Through eyes that focus as Thine own—
Not on the outer silhouette of flesh,
But deep inside the muscle and the bone.

Lord, help me hear as Thou dost hear,
Not just the sound of words alone,
But rather, hear the inner cry for help
That springs from needs too deep to make
    them known.

Then let me be an instrument
That, in Thy skilled and wise control,
May speak or be in some kind, loving way,
The means through which Thy strength restores
    their soul.

Share Your Faith

Share your faith in the Lord Jesus Christ;
    There are those who have not heard.
Then share your faith in the Lord Jesus Christ
    That they may know your Lord.
Tell them what He's done for you;
    Tell them Jesus loves them too.
Oh, speak a word to others,
    And share your faith.

Live Not in Vain

He rowed his boat across the lake;
He passed from shore to shore.
The ripple quickly disappeared;
The lake was still once more.

Another built a bridge across
To reach the other side;
He took the time to build it well,
To make it strong and wide.

So all who followed after him,
With thankful hearts, could say,
"A wise and faithful man has passed
Before us on the way."

When I have crossed the lake of life
And step on heaven's shore,
Will there remain some earthly sign
That I have passed before?

Have I so lived that other men,
Who follow in my train,
Will find the way to heaven's shore,
Or have I lived in vain?

The Divine Author

Our memories, like pages of a book,
Stand vigil on the bookshelf of the mind.
The pages are all written one by one.
The author pens the story by design.
One page alone does not the story tell.
Each chapter has a purpose, showing, when
The book has been completed, page by page,
How skillful was the writer with his pen.
Our memories at first show no design,
But if we let the Author have His way,
He, who knows and doeth all things well,
Will write the pages wisely day by day,
So when, at last, the final page is penned,
Our book of memories complete some day;
The things that we have let the Author write,
Will then determine what the book can say.

The Old, Old Story

There is an old, old story
Of unseen things above,
Of Jesus and His glory,
Of Jesus and His love;
I love to tell the story,
For some have never heard
The message of salvation,
From God's own holy Word.
They, too, must hear this story.
O God of grace and glory,
Help me to tell the story
Of Jesus and His love!

I love to read the Bible,
God's Word to all mankind;
Within its sacred pages,
The love of God I find.
But some have never read it,
The message of God's Son;
This story of salvation,
Was meant for everyone.
By life and conversation
I'll tell His great salvation
Till every tongue and nation
Has heard of Jesus' love.

I love to sing the story,
My song shall ever be
Of praise and adoration
To Him who died for me.
But many sit in silence,
They have no song to sing,
Unless I go and tell them
Of Christ my Lord and King.
With great anticipation
I'll sing of His salvation,
Till every man and nation
Can sing this joyful song.

Approved of God

The gift of time is mine to spend
    However I may please.
The choice is mine—to spend my days
    In service or in ease.

The gift of strength is mine to spend
    On things that I think best;
'Tis mine alone, for loss or gain,
    To squander or invest.

O giver of each perfect gift,
    Give wisdom now I pray,
To wisely spend the time and strength
    Allotted me today.

To be approved of God—my highest goal;
    To be approved of God—with all my soul.
I long to hear Him say,
    As Jesus turns my way,
These words on judgment day,
    "My child, well done."

He May Need You

The longest bridge may yet be built,
The fastest plane be flown;
The tallest building's architect,
As yet, may be unknown.

The greatest song may yet be penned;
The greatest speech be made,
The greatest book unpublished, still;
The largest deal be made.

A weaver may yet be unborn,
To weave the finest rug,
A scientist be working now
On some new wonder drug.

31

Some artist, by his paint and skill,
May find within his mind
A thing of beauty yet unseen,
The finest of its kind.

The fastest race may yet be run,
The longest jump be made,
The highest mountain yet be climbed,
The students' highest grade.

And so, my child, remember this:
There's much yet to be done.
God made you for some special task
And saved you by His Son.

So venture out in His great strength,
And with Him as your guide,
Seek wisdom, skill and open doors,
And trust Him to provide.

There is no task too big for Him!
Perhaps He'll choose to do
Some deed of greatness for mankind
And want the likes of you.

No Greater Joy

There is no greater joy than serving Jesus.
    There is no greater joy than working for Him.
Wherever He leads,
    Whatever He needs,
I'll gladly go and do.
    For there is no greater joy than serving the Lord.

If you are young and looking for action,
    Genuine joy and deep satisfaction,
Here is the way to build a life that really counts
    For now and eternity!
There is no greater joy than spending your life
        for Him.
    It's a wonderful, wonderful life to be serving
        the Lord.

Lord, I Lift Up Mine Eyes

Lord, I lift up mine eyes,
Lord, I lift up mine eyes.
I look on the fields of the world
And see the harvest is white.

Lord, I lift up mine eyes,
Lord, I lift up mine eyes
And learn of Thy love for the world,
Revealed on Calvary's cross.

Lord, I lift up mine eyes,
Lord, I lift up mine eyes
And pray that my love for the world
May grow to be more like Thine own.

Missions

That Every Man Should Know

I wonder where the people went
    That Jesus bid to go
And tell the gospel message so
    That every man should know.

Then Peter and Paul and others, too,
    Went preaching through the land
To tell the world of Jesus' love,
    Obeying His command.

But now two thousand years have passed,
    And millions do not know
That Jesus died on Calvary
    To save them from their woe.

I do not know why some have failed
    To heed His word and go;
But Lord, help me to faithful be,
    That every man should know.

Empty Hands

Empty hands that reach for someone
Who can help them in their plight,
    Who can tell them of salvation,
Who can point them to the Light.
    Empty hands, empty hands, do I see,
    do I see.

Empty hearts that long for something
That will satisfy their soul,
Bring them peace and satisfaction,
Cleanse their sins and make them whole.
Empty hearts, empty hearts, do I see,
do I see.

Empty lives that have no meaning,
Searching vainly for a goal;
Life to them is but a treadmill,
With no purpose in their soul.
Empty lives, empty lives, do I see,
do I see.

We must tell them of the Saviour
Who their emptiness can fill,
Who can satisfy their longing
And their deepest needs fulfill.
Empty hands, empty hearts, empty lives,
do I see.

Until

Until the pages of God's Word
Are held in every hand,
Until the knowledge of God's love
Is known in every land;
Until at last we have fulfilled
The Saviour's last command,
Our task is not complete, my friend.
Our task is not complete!

Until each man with his own eyes
Can read salvation's plan,
Until in his own tongue he hears,
So he can understand;
Until within his heart he knows
That God loves ev'ry man,
Our task is not complete, my friend.
Our task is not complete!

Until the tongue of ev'ry man
Can pray in Jesus' name,
And ask forgiveness for his sin,
Confessing guilt and blame;
Until the heart of ev'ry man,
God's promises can claim.
Our task is not complete, my friend.
Our task is not complete!

Does Jesus Care?

Does Jesus care that men in fear
    Bow down to gods of stone,
Not knowing yet that peace of heart
    Is found in Christ alone?

Does Jesus care that lost men pray
    To gods that cannot hear,
To gods that cannot sense their need
    Or take away their fear?

Does Jesus care that lost men dance
    Before their gods in vain;
To earn forgiveness for their sin,
    To ease their inner pain?

Yes, Jesus cares, and we must care
Enough to let them know
The living Son of God now waits
To save them from their woe.

Stir Me, Lord

Stir me, Lord, that I may see
Beyond my selfish greed
To those for whom the Saviour died,
A world in desperate need.

Stir me, Lord, that I may hear
Above the noisy din
The pleading voice of those who need
Salvation from their sin.

Stir me, Lord, that I may do
My part in Thy great plan,
To spread the gospel message till
It reaches every man.

Stir me, Lord, Oh, stir me!
Till in my heart I find
Compassion like unto Thine own,
Embracing all mankind.

Compassion

A heart of deep compassion,
O Lord, for this I plead;
That when I look at others,
My heart will sense their need.
Then let me be a mirror,
Reflecting from above,
The person of my Saviour,
His power and His love.
Compassion, Lord, for others,
Oh, grant it, Lord, I pray,
For millions 'cross the ocean
And those I meet today.

Compassion, Lord, for others,
This is my great desire;
Within my heart now kindle
A holy, selfless fire.
A passion, Lord, for people
That have not heard His name,
That Jesus died to save them
Or even that He came.
Compassion, Lord, to stir me
Until my life shall be
A sacred, burning altar
Of service, Lord, for Thee.

Compassion, Lord, for others,
Enough, if You should ask
That I should leave my homeland
To do some special task.
A deep and holy passion
To gladly answer yes,
That in the light of Calv'ry
My heart could do no less.
A heart of deep compassion
Create in me I pray,
And I will gladly follow
As You point out the way.

How Long?

How long since you prayed for a servant of God
In some foreign land, proclaiming God's Word?
How long since in love you have prayed for his
    health,
Remembered his needs and have shared of your
    wealth?

How long has it been since you knelt down to pray
For a friend serving Christ in a land far away?
How long since you wrote to encourage his heart,
To tell him you pray and are doing your part?

How long will it be 'til the battle is done,
The praying is past, the vict'ry is won?
It may not be long, but you still have today
To reach out in love as you faithfully pray.

Where Is Love?

Pleading lips are asking,
  "Where is love, where is love?"
Pleading lips are asking,
  "Where is love, where is love?"
Are there ears to hear them pleading?
  Is there someone who is heeding
Those whose lips are pleading, pleading?
  "Where is love, where is love?"

Searching eyes are watching
  For some love, for some love.
Searching eyes are watching
  For some love, for some love.
Is the light of love now glowing
  So that searching eyes, not knowing,
Clearly see God's love now showing?
  There is love, there is love.

Praise the name of Jesus,
  He is love, He is love!
Praise the name of Jesus,
  He is love, He is love!
No more searching, no more pleading
  For the love they could be heeding;
Christ is all that they are needing.
  He is love, He is love!

Would You Have an Answer?

I dreamed that I went to a faraway land
   Where the gospel had never been heard.
I gathered the people around me to tell
   The story from God's Holy Word.
I told them how Jesus had died for their sin,
   The story of love we all know;
But when I had finished, they sadly replied,
   "Why did you not come long ago?
Why did you not come long ago?
   Why did you not come long ago?"
But when I had finished, they sadly replied,
   "Why did you not come long ago?"

I dreamed once again that in heaven I stood,
   And Jesus was talking with me.
He showed me His nailprints, then sadly He said,
   "These wounds, are they nothing to thee?
I asked you to tell all the world of My love,
   But still there are millions unsaved.
My death on the cross still means nothing to them;
   They carry their sin to their grave.
These wounds, are they nothing to thee?
   These wounds, are they nothing to thee?"
He showed me His nailprints, then sadly He said,
   "These wounds, are they nothing to thee?"

Ah, yes! It was only a dream that I had,
   But what if it really were true?
Would you have an answer to give them, my
     friend,
   If questions like these came to you?
Thank God for the time He is giving to us,
   To tell a lost world of His grace;

Then let us go quickly and tell the Good News
    And pray that we reach ev'ry race.
If questions like these came to you,
    If questions like these came to you,
Would you have an answer to give them, my
        friend,
    If questions like these came to you?

Why Must I Die?

Why must I die? Is there no one to help me?
Is there no way to save my dying soul?
Is there no plan wherein there is salvation?
Or must I die? Must sin then take its toll?

Why must I die? My heart cries out in anguish;
The weight of sin is more than I can bear.
By day and night the fear of death o'erwhelms me.
Why must I die? Is there not one to care?

Why must I die? Is there not someone somewhere
Who knows a way to free my soul from sin?
Is there no ear to hear my pleas for mercy?
Why must I die? Is there no peace within?

Why must I die? Oh, could it be that somewhere
There is a God of whom I have not heard
Eternal life already has provided?
But I must die, for I have not been told!

"Why must I die? Why must I die?"
Can we not hear the heathen cry?
Or will they perish, still in darkness pleading,
"Why must I die? Why must I die?"

What If We Quit?

What if we quit? Who will bear the Good News?
Spread the glad message if we should refuse?
We must go forth; there is no other way:
Let us press on without further delay.

What if we quit when the way becomes hard?
Rugged and rough was the path of our Lord.
Bitter the cup which He drank for our sake:
He did not quit, nor His mission forsake.

What if we quit? Have we counted the cost?
Men in their sins are eternally lost.
Jesus has died their salvation to win:
Still they will perish and die in their sin.

What if we quit? Can we not hear the cry
Rising from souls who are fearful to die?
How can we carelessly heed not their plea?
Voices are calling to you and to me.

Lord of the Harvest, we go at Thy Word,
Spreading the gospel till all men have heard;
Promised Thy pow'r to defeat ev'ry foe,
Promised Thy presence as onward we go.

The Sacrifice

The heathen bow before their gods
  Of clay and wood and stone
And vainly offer sacrifice
  That will for sin atone.
Must they forever sacrifice
  Before a heathen god,
Not knowing Jesus died for them
  And shed His precious blood?

Somewhere a heathen soul bows down
  And makes a sacrifice
To seek forgiveness for his sin
  And prays it will suffice.
He does not know that Jesus died
  To pay the price for sin,
That Jesus by His sacrifice
  Forgiveness thus did win.

The sacrifice for sin was made
  At such an awful cost,
But if the heathen do not hear,
  Their souls will still be lost.
Then let us hasten with the news
  That Jesus died for sin;
His sacrifice is heaven's gate,
  And they may enter in.

The Greatest Story Is Yet Untold

Look to a people who still have not heard
One single portion of God's Holy Word.
Salvation, too, has for them been procured,
But they must the story be told.

Look to a village where Christ is not known.
See men bow down before idols of stone,
Seeking relief found in Jesus alone.
They must the story be told.

Wandering nomads in tents made of skin,
Telling their fables by candlelight dim,
Never once hearing the story of Him.
They must the story be told.

Think of the souls we must face in that day,
Those who have died without knowing the way.
What will we do when they stand up and say,
"Why is it we were not told?"

When in the judgment before Him we stand,
Knowing full well the redemption He planned,
What shall we say when we hear His demand:
"Why was the story not told?"

The Saviour has bid us to tell the Good News;
Then let us obey Him, let no one refuse
To tell it abroad until all men have heard
The world's greatest story as told in God's Word.

So Much to Do

So much to do, Lord,
Until all have heard
　Salvation's story
From Thy precious Word.
　Come in Thy power
And fill me, I pray;
　Fit me for service
And use me this day.

So little time, Lord,
So soon they will die,
　Quickly, too quickly
The days hasten by.
　Lord, I can see
That the harvest is white;
　Where are the reapers?
Soon cometh the night!

Laborers are few and
The harvest is great,
　Now we must reach them
Before it's too late.
　Be Thou my guide and
My strength as I go,
　Seeking to reach men
In sin and in woe.

So little time, Lord,
　　And so much to do;
So great the harvest,
　　The laborers so few.
Help me, Lord Jesus,
　　In service to be
Faithful and useful
　　Each moment for Thee.

Move Me

Move me, Lord, to pray
For those who preach Thy Word;
Who bear the gospel of Thy grace
To those who have not heard.

Move me, Lord, to give
Of all that I possess
That heathen souls might come to know
Thy perfect righteousness.

Move me, Lord, to go!
My life I freely give
To bear the news if Thou should'st choose,
That dying souls might live.

Move me, Lord, Oh, move me!
I give my all to Thee
To use just where and when and how,
That blinded eyes may see.

Let Us Press On

Over and over and over again
 The story to some has been told,
While others still wait without once having heard
 Of Jesus and blessings untold.

Why should we keep on returning to those
 Who've heard it so often before,
While some never once ever heard of His love?
 Yet these we so often ignore.

Witnessing always to those we are near,
 Repeating God's message of grace.
But we must press on as we pray, give and go,
 Until we have reached ev'ry race.

Let us press on! Oh, let us press on,
 Bearing His precious Word;
Telling the story of Christ and His love
 To those who never have heard.

I Wonder Why

I think of those for whom Christ died,
 Who still have never heard;
Who do not know of God's great love,
 Recorded in His Word:
And wonder why, and wonder why
 They still have never heard.

I think of people lost in sin
  Who sit in darkness still
Because no light has come to them,
  This cannot be God's will;
And wonder why, and wonder why
  They sit in darkness still.

I think of us who have the light;
  But still have failed to share
The message of the grace of God,
  His love beyond compare;
And wonder why, and wonder why,
  We still have failed to share.

Lord, thoughts are not enough, I see,
  Some action must begin.
Send me, I pray, with light to those
  In darkness and in sin.
In thy great strength, Lord, now I go,
  The action to begin.

How Much Are You Involved?

The risen Saviour gave this last command,
  To take the gospel into every land;
But millions still the story do not know,
  For we have failed to heed His word to go.

Why do we wait, why do we still delay?
  Oh, let us hasten now His word obey
And carry out the work that He has planned,
  To reach the lost in ev'ry tribe and land.

The task is great, we all must do our part,
　　Become involved and work with all our heart;
Until His word is known in ev'ry land
　　And we've fulfilled the Saviour's last command.

Are you involved in sending forth the gospel?
　　Are you involved in giving out His Word?
Are you obeying Jesus' Great Commission?
　　The question comes, "How much are you
　　　involved?"

Help Me, Lord

Help me, Lord, to share the gospel.
There are those for whom Christ died
Still in darkness, waiting, waiting
For the light I could provide.

Help me, Lord, to share the gospel.
There are those who hunger still
For the Bread of Life from heaven.
Jesus could their hunger fill.

Help me, Lord, to share the gospel
With the thirsty souls who wait,
Wait for Christ the Living Water.
Help me, lest I go too late!

Help me, Lord, to share the gospel.
Make me bold to bear the news;
Fill me with the Holy Spirit;
Use me when and where You choose.

Go Ye! Go Ye!

Go ye! Go ye! into all the world;
    Reaching ev'ry land
With the gospel message.
    This is God's command.
Do not linger any longer,
    For the need is great;
Fields are white, are white to harvest,
    Soon 'twill be too late.

Hasten, then, ye soldiers of the cross,
    Now His Word obey;
Take to all the gospel,
    Go without delay.
Go ye! Go ye!
    Was the Master's last command.
With the gospel message,
    Reaching ev'ry land.

I am with you always,
    Anywhere you go;
This is God's own promise,
    We need fear no foe.
Reaching forth to ev'ry nation,
    Till all have heard the love of God;
Walking paths of service
    No one else has trod.

Hasten, then, ye soldiers of the cross,
　　Now His Word obey;
Take to all the gospel,
　　Go without delay.
Do not linger any longer,
　　For the need is great;
Fields are white, are white to harvest,
　　Soon 'twill be too late.

Forgiveness

The heathen kneel before their gods
　　That cannot see or hear,
To seek forgiveness for their sin
　　And freedom from their fear.
If they should pray until they die,
　　No answer would be theirs;
A graven image cannot save
　　Or even hear their prayers.

Then we who know the one true God
　　Who lives and answers prayer
And grants forgiveness for our sin
　　And freedom from despair,
Must pass the message on to them
　　Before it is too late.
Ten thousand souls may die in sin
　　If we should hesitate.

O living God, help us, we pray,
  To make the message known
To those who still have never seen
  The love which thou hast shown,
Till ev'ry man on earth has heard
  Forgiveness comes from Thee,
And some are saved from ev'ry tribe
  To live eternally!

Everywhere That Men Are Dwelling

Westward rise the lofty mountains,
  Eastward lie the desert sands;
Northward see the lakes and forests,
  Southward are the jungle lands.
Everywhere that men are dwelling,
  We must go at God's command;
Telling them the gospel message,
  Preaching Christ in ev'ry land.

Ev'ry language must be mastered,
  Ev'ry ear must hear His Word;
All must understand the gospel,
  Go till all the world has heard.
Sharing Christ with those around us,
  Then with those in other lands;
Reaching ev'ry tongue and nation
  This is what His Word demands.

Go to cities with their millions,
    Farm and village homes as well;
Jungle huts and tents of nomads,
    Ev'rywhere that people dwell.
Black or brown or white or yellow,
    Jesus died for all the same;
Ev'ry tribe and ev'ry nation
    Must be reached in Jesus' name.

Couriers for Christ

There's a message in the Word of God for all men
    ev'rywhere,
That will cleanse them from their sin and set them
    free;
But the King has sent the message, not by angels
    from above,
For the task has been assigned to you and me.

There is pardon for the sinner who will place his
    faith in Christ,
There's redemption at the cross for ev'ry man.
Let us bear the blessed news the King entrusted
    unto us.
Let us go and preach His Name in ev'ry land!

There is peace of heart for those who live in fear
    and guilt and shame.
There is rest for souls in turmoil from their sin.
Hasten! messengers of peace, a troubled world
    awaits the news,
"Christ can change your life and give you peace
    within."

We are couriers with a message from the King.
Let us hasten to carry His Word
To the people who never have heard
Of the message of peace and pardon from the King.

Awake, O Church

Awake, O church, and face the task!
Our mission is not done,
Until we preach in ev'ry land
The message of God's Son.

To ev'ry tribe and ev'ry tongue
The message must be plain,
That Jesus died to save their souls,
Or Christ has died in vain.

The task is great, the laborers few,
The fields already white.
No longer wait, lest some should die,
All are precious in His sight.

What could we say if we should stand
Before the judgment seat,
And Christ should ask a reason why
Our task is not complete?

O God, we gladly give ourselves
And all that we possess.
Now take control, Thy work complete;
How can we offer less?

A Glorious Task

Do you see them over yonder,
Those who have no gospel light;
Searching, searching for salvation,
Can you see them in their plight?

Do you hear their pleading voices?
"Come and help us or we die!"
They have never heard the gospel.
Can you hear them as they cry?

Do you hear the voice of Jesus?
"Look! The harvest fields are white."
Who will go and reap the harvest?
Daylight soon will turn to night.

Let us hasten with the gospel.
Some must go and bear the news.
All can pray and give to send them.
Surely no one can refuse.

Do not linger any longer.
Hasten now without delay.
We must tell them of salvation.
To the work while yet 'tis day.

'Tis a glorious task to give them the gospel,
Those who as yet have not heard.
'Tis a glorious task to tell them of Jesus,
Tell them of God and His Word.

Unless We Go

Unless we go to all mankind,
According to the plan
That God conceived in His own mind
Before the world began;
Unless the finished work of Christ
Is told to every man,
Salvation's plan for sinful man
Will still unfinished be.

Unless the ear of every man
Has heard the joyful sound,
That true forgiveness for his sin
Within God's Word is found;
And that the prayer of faith in Christ
Will start him heaven bound,
Salvation's plan for sinful man
Will still unfinished be.

Unless each tribe and ev'ry tongue
Can read God's written Word;
Unless the story of God's grace
By ev'ry man is heard;
Unless God's Spirit through His Word,
In ev'ry heart has stirred,
Salvation's plan for sinful man,
Will still unfinished be.

Go Forth

Go forth, go forth for Jesus,
All ye who love the Lord,
And take the gospel message
To those who have not heard.
The Saviour will go with you,
To conquer ev'ry foe;
It is His great desire,
That all His grace should know.

Go forth, go forth on pathways
That no one else has trod;
To tell of peace and pardon,
To tell the love of God.
Why should we tell the story
To some men o'er and o'er,
While millions now are dying,
That have not heard before?

Go forth, go forth in power.
We must not hesitate.
Today we still may reach them;
Tomorrow is too late.
Since Jesus bid us reach them,
Two thousand years have passed;
The work is still unfinished,
We must complete the task.

Go forth, go forth and conquer,
Be strong against the foe;
For Jesus is our leader,
And He has bid us go.
We serve a risen Saviour,
Victorious o'er the grave;
Who died and rose in triumph,
A sinful world to save.

The Good Samaritan

A man was beaten by some thieves,
And left alone to die;
Ignored by some who saw him there
But simply passed him by.
But with compassion in his heart,
A good Samaritan
Bound up his wounds with healing oil,
And took him to the inn.

If I should meet someone today,
Discouraged and in need;
Would I respond by helping him
With kindly word or deed?
Or would I choose to pass him by
And turn the other way?
How would I act? What would I do
If this occurred today?

If I should hear of some great need,
Perhaps across the sea,
Where Jesus' love is still not known,
What would my answer be?
Would I be willing there to go,
If that should be the test;
Or would I help to send someone,
If that would be the best?

O God, I want a heart that cares
For others that I meet;
For needs and people overseas,
And those across the street.

The Master Plan

O God, I read Thy Holy Word
And see Thy great design
To spread the news of Calv'ry love;
The task indeed is mine.

The master plan to reach the world
Began at Pentecost;
And now the Church must carry on,
Whatever be the cost.

This sacred trust is ours alone;
This is the only plan.
Though angels long to bear the news,
The task is left to man.

I must be faithful to my trust
Until the work is done
And I have done my part to spread
The message of God's Son.

Praying, Giving, Preaching

All may be faithful in praying,
Many be helpful by giving,
Some surely must go do the preaching
Till all men have heard the Good News.
Go ye! Go ye! Go into all the world.

Only One Plan

There's only one plan of redemption for man,
And we are a part of that plan;
To us has been given this story of love,
Our part is to reach ev'ry man.
This plan of redemption to save a lost world
Was formed in the mind of our God.
Salvation for all through Christ's death on
    the cross,
But the world must the story be told.

The price of the plan was the Father's own Son,
The dearest thing heaven could hold;
In infinite love He sent Jesus to die—
What a price to reclaim a lost world.
This plan of the ages required of the Son,
That He give His own self on a tree.
His lifeblood to shed for the sins of mankind,
That man, in his guilt, might go free.

God's part is complete; He is looking to you
To spread the glad message abroad;
If the world is to hear, if the story is told,
God's plan now depends upon you.
There's only one plan for the lost world to hear,
The message by us must go forth.
For we must tell others and they others still,
Till the story has covered the earth.

God's plan now depends upon you,
Yes, completely, depends upon you.
There's no other way that a lost world will know;
God's plan now depends upon you.

Ye Shall Be My Witnesses

Ye shall be my witnesses,
  Of ev'rything that I have said to you.
Ye shall be My witnesses
  Of all the things that ye have seen Me do.
Go witness to all people
  With power from above;
Tell them of salvation,
  Of mercy, grace and love.

To those who sit in darkness,
  Who wander in the night,
Go tell of My salvation;
  I am this dark world's Light.
To those who seek atonement
  From gods of wood and stone,
Go tell them that forgiveness
  Is found in Me alone.

To those who still are hungry,
    Who never have been fed,
Go tell them I can fill them;
    I am the Living Bread.
To those who still are thirsty
    And never satisfied,
Go take the living water
    That I alone provide.

Go witness to all people
    With power from above;
Tell them of salvation,
    Of mercy, grace and love.
Then ye shall be My witnesses,
    Fulfilling all I have commanded you to do.

Consecration

A Living Sacrifice

O God, I come before Thee now
   And on Thine altar lay
Myself, a living sacrifice,
   To serve Thee day by day.
Take all I am or hope to be
   And make it Thine today;
A living sacrifice I bring;
   Accept it, Lord, I pray.

I bring a living sacrifice;
   Myself, I offer Thee,
Made holy by the blood of Christ,
   Who died on Calvary.
My body, soul and spirit, Lord,
   I yield them all to Thee
That I might live in such a way
   That men see Christ in me.

I pledge Thee full allegiance, Lord,
   To live for Thee alone;
Oh take this living sacrifice,
   And use it as Thine own.
No longer self upon the throne,
   Let Christ be seen in me;
Work out Thy perfect will, O Lord,
   Whatever it may be.

A living sacrifice, I offer now to Thee.
   Oh take and use it, Lord,
Until Thy face I see;
   And then before Thy throne
My song shall ever be
   A sacrifice of praise to Thee.

A Cross

The mantles of sorrow which all men must wear,
  Ah, these are not crosses to bear.
A cross we must choose by an act of our will
  And seek its demands to fulfill.

My heartaches and sorrows and burdens and cares,
  Ah, these are not crosses to bear.
A cross I must choose by an act of my will
  And gladly my mission fulfill.

The cross Jesus carried, the grief that He bore,
  The crown full of thorns that He wore—
He could have escaped them, He need not have
    died;
  He chose to be thus crucified.

He need not have taken the way of the cross;
  The shame and reproach were not His.
No power could force Him to die in my place;
  He chose to with infinite grace.

By chance, if a cross I would bear for my Lord,
  Obey some command from His Word;
The task He assigns me may difficult be,
  But the choice will be left up to me.

Lord, Take My Life

Lord, take my life henceforth to be
  A living sacrifice for Thee;
As incense let my service rise
  To Thee, O God of earth and skies.

Lord, take my body as Thine own,
  And through it make Thy glory known;
Control my feet and heart and hands
  That they may move at Thy commands.

Lord, take my spirit and my soul,
  My inner self do Thou control;
My thoughts and motives purify,
  My self-deception crucify.

Take all I am and hope to be,
  That someday in eternity
The race of life that has been run
  May bring Thy cherished words, "Well done."

My Lord

Wherever You want me to go, my Lord,
At home or across the sea,
I'll go as You show me the way, my Lord;
I make now this prayer to Thee.

Whatever You want me to say, my Lord,
At home or across the sea,
I'll speak as You give me the words, my Lord;
I make now this prayer to Thee.

Whatever You want me to be, my Lord,
At home or across the sea,
I'll be by the grace that You give, my Lord;
I make now this prayer to Thee.

Lovest Thou Me More Than These?

Good things we have all around us,
Sent from the Father above;
Blessings poured out without measure
Come from His great heart of love.
Gratefully enter His presence,
Prayerfully go to our knees,
Quietly there hear Him saying,
"Lovest thou Me more than these?"

Those that we love all around us,
Precious the joys that we share;
Loved ones and friends close beside us,
Helping each burden to bear.
Tokens of God's loving-kindness,
Sent for our comfort and ease;
Listen! The Giver still asks thee,
"Lovest thou Me more than these?"

Life that's eternal in Jesus,
Heaven for all who believe;
Guidance on all of life's pathway,
Peace that the world cannot give.
Gifts from our Father in heaven,
Blessings that never shall cease;
Still, as His children, He asks us,
"Lovest thou Me more than these?"

The Blessed Hope

The World of Tomorrow

I know of a world that is lovely and fair,
A world that is free from all heartache and care;
No sickness and sorrow can follow me there
To my wonderful world of tomorrow.

I know of a world that has permanent peace,
A world where all hatred and fighting will cease,
A place where the fearful find blessed release
In this wonderful world of tomorrow.

I know of a world that is free from all sin,
A world where the wicked cannot enter in,
Where only the children of God may come in
To this wonderful world of tomorrow.

I know not just when this tomorrow will be,
But hope will someday turn to reality.
By faith I can see it is waiting for me,
This wonderful world of tomorrow.

The Best Is Yet to Come

So much of good has come my way
    Since first I found the Lord that day;
But even so, I still can say
    That the best is yet to come.

I felt the surge of joy within,
    When Jesus took away my sin;
In Him the heavenly joys begin,
    But the best is yet to come.

I know the peace that Jesus gives,
　　Within my heart contentment lives;
A precious gift of God it is,
　　But the best is yet to come.

Oh, the best is yet to come,
　　Yes, the best is yet to come;
On heaven's shore there'll be much more;
　　Yes, the best is yet to come.

But While We Wait

Christ will soon be coming—what a glorious day!
This His blessed promise when He went away.
Once by sinful man was slain,
Then He'll come a king to reign;
Now we wait His glad return.

What a resurrection when His own arise.
Saints from all the ages meeting in the skies;
Death forever banished there,
In that lovely land so fair;
Now we wait His glad return.

Then to see our Saviour, look upon His face;
Cast our crowns before Him, give Him rightful
　　place;
Thank Him for the love we've known,
Kneel to worship at His throne;
Now we wait His glad return.

He will come in power, sit upon His throne;
Setting up His kingdom, ruling with His own.
Once He came in lowly birth,
Then He'll come to rule the earth.
Now we wait His glad return.

But while we wait we will the vineyard keep.
But while we wait we must the harvest reap.
With anxious hearts we slumber not nor sleep,
But labor on while we the vigil keep.
We'll labor on while we wait.

The Bridegroom

When He comes on that great wedding day,
I'll be walking down the aisle
With axious eyes to see His face
And greet Him with a smile.

He'll come a kingly Bridegroom then,
All dressed in fine array.
With trumpet sound and angel voice
He'll catch His Bride away.

No thorny crown or cross this time.
A Saviour once He came
To make spotless garments for the Bride
Who would someday take His name.

This time in glory He will come,
A Bridegroom from above,
Who died and rose again to prove
His power and His love.

So as I walk this aisle of life,
I know that some glad day,
Perhaps real soon, He will return.
It could be yet today!

This precious hope refreshes me,
And I can sing a song;
Although the way is difficult,
It doesn't seem so long.

The aisle is leading me at last
To an altar in the sky,
Where I will join the one I love
To live with Him on high.

What a Wonderful, Wonderful Day

When days are filled with anxious care,
And blue skies turn to gray;
The blessed hope of His return
Sustains me on my way.

When days of disappointment come,
And shadows cross my way;
I ponder His return for me
And then with joy I say,

What a wonderful, wonderful day it will be,
When Jesus returns in His glory;
To take us away, oh glorious day,
We'll live in His presence forever.
What a wonderful, wonderful day it will be,
Oh, come let us shout the glad story.
In power and love, He'll come from above
On that wonderful, wonderful, glorious day.
What a wonderful day it will be!

The Blessed Hope

What can cheer the saddened heart,
   Cause the sorrow to depart?
What can cause a song to start?
   The blessed, blessed hope of His return.

What can make the day worthwhile,
   Turn a frown into a smile,
Gladden every weary mile?
   The blessed, blessed hope of His return.

What can brighten up your day,
   Give new courage on your way,
Help sustain you when you pray?
   The blessed, blessed hope of His return.

TRUST in God's Ability

Nothing Is Impossible

I read in the Bible the promise of God,
That nothing for Him is too hard.
Impossible things He has promised to do
If we faithfully trust in His Word.

The Word of the Lord is an anchor secure
When winds of uncertainty blow;
Though man in his weakness may falter and fail,
His Word will not fail us we know.

"All things are possible," this is His Word.
Receive it, 'tis written for you.
Believe in His promises; God cannot fail;
For what He has said He will do.

Creator of all things, with infinite pow'r,
He spoke—they appeared by His mouth.
Impossible things are not known unto Him.
He made us, He ruleth the earth.

Nothing is impossible when you put your trust in
    God;
Nothing is impossible when you're trusting in His
    Word.
Hearken to the voice of God to thee:
    "Is there anything too hard for Me?"
Then put your trust in God alone and rest upon
    His Word;
For ev'rything, oh ev'rything, yes ev'rything is
    possible with God!

God Cannot Make a Mistake

Rejoice in the knowledge that One from above,
Whose essence is power and wisdom and love,
Will help those who ask Him, each problem to
    solve,
And He cannot make a mistake.

Although there is much we do not understand,
And cannot explain all the things He has planned;
Enough, if we know we are led by His hand,
For He cannot make a mistake.

Oh, Christian, remember that God on His Throne
Has promised forever to care for His own.
"I will not forsake thee, nor leave thee alone."
And He cannot make a mistake.

We fear not the future since God knows the way,
And dread not the problems that vex us today.
By trusting the Saviour, your fears He'll allay,
For He cannot make a mistake.

Why Not Ask God for a Miracle?

We say the power of our God
    Can hang the world in space.
We say in love He sent His Son
    To suffer in our place.
We say the Bible says all this,
    And surely this is true;
Then when we pray, why should we doubt
    What God can really do?

We say that Jesus conquered death
    And rose up from the dead.
We say He will return again
    To earth just as He said.
We say the Bible says all this,
    And surely this is true;
Then let this risen, coming King
    Reveal what He can do!

Why not ask God to do a miracle for you?
    Let God be God and really prove what He can do!
For He is either God of all,
    Or He is no God at all,
Why not ask God to do a miracle for you?

I Know Who Holds the Future

I do not know what lies ahead,
The way I cannot see;
Yet one stands near to be my guide;
He'll show the way to me.

I do not know how many days
Of life are mine to spend,
But one who knows and cares for me
Will keep me to the end.

I do not know the course ahead,
What joys and griefs are there;
But one is near who fully knows;
I'll trust His loving care.

Secure

Once I feared to face the morrow,
Feared the things that it might bring;
Watched for something to rely on,
Something safe, secure and strong.

Then I found in Christ the Saviour,
One in whom I felt secure;
God Himself to guide my pathway,
Nothing else could be more sure.

Oh, the joy of knowing Jesus,
Oh, the peace of mind He brings;
Now secure in Him I'm resting,
Daily now my glad heart sings.

Secure in Christ I walk along life's pathway;
Secure in Christ I journey day by day.
With God Himself as my divine protection,
I am secure, no need to fear the way.

In God We Trust

In God we trust and fear no foe;
Take courage and be strong.
We walk by faith and not by sight,
And sing the victor's song.

In God we trust—He rules the world;
Then let the nations rage.
His mighty power will remain
The same from age to age.

In God we trust and sing for joy,
His kingdom shall not fail.
The King of kings and Lord of lords
Will over all prevail.

In God we trust and bless His name;
Eternal God is He.
When earth and heaven pass away,
He still our God will be.

In God we trust and follow Him;
Unfailing guide is He.
He knows the path that lies ahead;
The future He can see.

In God we trust—He lives today,
Triumphant over death.
In glory He'll return one day
To reign upon the earth.

His love forever is our stay.
His wisdom guides us on our way.
His power keeps us day by day.
In God we trust.

Give God a Chance

The power of God we all can trace,
In earth and sea and outer space;
But still He wants to prove in you
The miracles that He can do.

The love of God, for all to see,
Was clearly shown at Calvary;
But now He wants to show anew
How much He really cares for you.

His wisdom planned the universe
And guides the planets in their course.
He wants to guide your pathway, too,
And plan the life that's best for you.

Give God a chance, His wisdom will not fail;
Give God a chance, His goodness shall prevail.
Put off thy doubts, and trust Him, come what may;
Give God a chance, His power to display.

To Those Who Believe

A blind man sat beside the road
As Jesus passed that way.
He loudly cried, "Have mercy, Lord,
And give me sight, I pray."
Then Jesus heard his cry for aid
And honored his belief;
This blind man came in simple faith
And found complete relief.

So men today have sought His help
And found Him able still
To do things thought impossible,
Their deepest needs fulfill.
But now, as then, the answer comes
To those alone who pray,
In simple faith, believing Christ
Will always make a way.

A father asked the Lord one day
To heal his little lad.
He hardly dared to ask for help,
So little faith he had.
Then Jesus said, "If you believe,
Then all things can be done!"
He answered, "Lord, I do believe!"
And Jesus healed his son.

If you, my friend, have found some need
Impossible to meet;
Then come in prayer with trusting faith,
And bow at Jesus' feet.
Whatever your request may be,
Believe Him as you pray;
With Him all things are possible,
He's still the same today.

Praise, Testimony and Victory

What Can I Bring?

How can I praise Him?
What can He want from me—
He, who but did speak
To make the land and sea?
Is there not something
That He could not create,
Some gift to bring Him?
Why do I hesitate?
I can bring Him love,
For this is born of choice.
No robot speaking,
However clear the voice,
Responds in true love,
For its design is set.
Love acts in freedom,
Chancing joy or regret.
This gift I bring then,
My praise that springs from love,
Rising up on wings
Of prayer to God above.

What a Salvation

Yesterday's guilt can condemn me no more.
Gone is the sin that enchained me before.
Jesus has died for the sins of the past,
Paid is the penalty—freedom at last!

Today there is victory over all sin.
Daily the peace of God ruleth within.
Broken the power of sin in my life,
Gone is the tumult, frustration and strife.

Tomorrow I'll flee from the presence of sin,
No more temptation without or within.
Sickness and sorrow and death passed away,
Oh, what a future awaits me some day!

Saved from sin's penalty—free from the past!
Saved from sin's power—now vict'ry at last!
Saved from sin's presence some day I shall be.
What a salvation He purchased for me!

That He Might Be Glorified

Saved from sin, God's grace has wrought it;
None could else be justified;
Jesus only paid the ransom
That He might be glorified.

Yielding fully to the Saviour,
Walking daily by His side,
Trusting Him to lead us always
That He may be glorified.

Serving Jesus—oh, how blessed!
Telling men why Jesus died,
Pointing them to God's salvation
That He may be glorified.

Saved from sin—oh, hallelujah!
Yielded fully to our Guide,
We will serve where'er He leads us
That He may be glorified.

Liberation

Walls of fear surrounded me;
 A prisoner was I,
Imprisoned by my guilt and shame,
 Afraid to live or die.
But then I heard of Him who came
 To set the prisoner free,
To liberate mankind from sin
 Through death on Calvary.

Once I lived for self alone,
 A slave of foolish pride;
I deeply drank from Pleasure's cup,
 But was not satisfied.
But now I am a son of God,
 No slave to self and sin;
With liberation's power now,
 Christ lives and reigns within.

Self once formed a prison wall,
 Confining me inside;
Escape I could not from my greed,
 My envy and my pride.
The walls fell down and freedom came
 When Jesus entered in,
With liberating love He came
 To conquer self and sin.

I've found liberation at last,
 Unshackled am I from the past;
From sin and from self I am free.
 Christ gave liberation to me.

Until That Day

I wish that I could write a song
With such a melody
That all the world could join and sing
In perfect harmony.

I wish that I could pen some words
That men of every race
Could understand and join to sing
Of God's redeeming grace.

Then men from everywhere on earth
Could form a choir and sing
The praises due to Jesus Christ,
Our Saviour, Lord and King.

But since this cannot be, I know,
I'll praise Him with my heart
Until that heavenly choir is formed,
And I can have a part.

The Master's Touch

The hand that drew creation's plan,
And placed the breath of life in man;
That healed the sick and made them whole,
Reached down in love and touched my soul.

Once shackled by the chains of sin,
No hope without, no peace within;
The Master's touch brought full release,
My restless soul found perfect peace.

The One whose power raised the dead,
And gave five thousand people bread;
Who bade the wind and waves depart,
Has come and touched my sinful heart.

How wonderful this change in me,
A miracle—how can it be
That God Himself, in love divine,
Would come and touch this heart of mine!

He touched me and suddenly all was changed,
And in that moment I found a new life divine!
In faith I spoke His name, in grace the Saviour
       came,
And suddenly all was changed.

Our Worship and Our Praise

Almighty God, we come
   With heart and voice to raise
Before Thee now in word and song
   Our worship and our praise.

We lift our hearts in praise,
   In spirit now draw nigh;
Like incense let our worship rise
   Before Thy throne on high.

We praise Thee for Thy Word,
   Thy truth—it will not fail;
Though heaven and earth should pass away,
   Thy Word shall still prevail.

Come join us in our song
  Of praise to God above,
Who by His Son and written Word
  Has shown to us His love.

My Creed

  I believe that Jesus died for me;
I believe He paid sin's penalty;
  He conquered death and sin
When He arose again.
  And now He lives within;
This, I believe.

I've Found a New Life in Jesus

I've found a new life in Jesus,
The old things have all passed away;
Awakened, I rose up to enter
The dawn of an unending day.

I've found a new life in Jesus,
My values in life are all new;
Eternal things now fill my vision,
The earthly have faded from view.

I've found a new life in Jesus,
I'm walking by faith not by sight;
He strengthens my heart in the daytime,
And gives me a song in the night.

I've found a new life in Jesus,
The pleasures of sin will not do;
My heart demands something more lasting,
My soul must be satisfied too.

I've found a new life in Jesus,
To please Him is all my delight;
I now have a purpose for living,
My hope for the future is bright.

I've found a new life in Jesus,
My world of tomorrow looks bright;
The darkness that once did surround me
Is lost in its heavenly light.

I Do Not Understand

I do not understand why God would want to come
    to earth,
Or why He chose to come to us by such a lowly
    birth.
A wretched stable—what a place for Jesus to
    appear.
The King of kings and Lord of lords stooped down
    to meet man here.

I do not understand the love that prompted
    Calvary,
Or why He chose to bear such shame upon a cursed
    tree.
A greater love than this? Ah, no! What more could
    He have done
Than give His life upon the cross to prove His love
    to man?

I do not understand how Christ could conquer
    death and hell,
Or how the prophets long ago could this event
    foretell.
But from the tomb He came that day, ere dawned
    the morning light,
For all the world to see and know His power and
    His might.

But this I know, He did all this and more
To open wide salvation's door.
It is His Word! On this I firmly stand;
Just why and how, I need not understand.

I do not understand how Christ, descending from
    the sky,
Can take His own to dwell with Him in mansions
    up on high,
Nor how forever we can live in never-ending bliss.
Eternal life! How can it be? Yet He has promised
    this.

But this I know, He will return one day,
And catch His chosen ones away.
It is His Word! On this I firmly stand;
Just why and how, I need not understand.

I Believe

I believe that Jesus died,
    On the cross was crucified,
All the debt for sin supplied—
    This I believe,
    This I believe.

I believe He rose again,
    Victor over death and sin,
My salvation thus to win—
    This I believe,
    This I believe.

Be Strong in the Lord

Do temptations molest you as you journey on the
    way?
Not a one can overcome you if you look to Him
    each day.
Be strong in the Lord!

Are you weakened in the battle by some hidden
    doubt or fear?
When you trust in Him completely, all your doubts
    will disappear.
Be strong in the Lord!

When I come to the battle, in my weakness I
    would fail.
But in Christ I now can conquer, for His power
    will prevail.
Be strong in the Lord!

It Makes a Lot of Difference

It makes a lot of diff'rence
    When you're doing it for the Lord,
It makes a lot of diff'rence
    When you do it for someone you love.
And when you get to heaven,
    There will be a great reward.
Yes, it makes a lot of diff'rence
    When you're doing it for the Lord.
It makes a lot of diff'rence
    When you do it for the Lord.

The Life and
Work of Christ

When I Remember

Sometimes I feel like cryin'
    When I remember Jesus praying in Gethsemane
And know He shed for me great drops of blood.
    Oh, what agonizing prayer the Saviour must
      have suffered there.

Sometimes I feel like cryin'
    When I remember how my Saviour was betrayed
      by all
In dark Gethsemane, in Pilate's hall.
    Oh, alone He stood, without a friend to help
      and comfort Him.

Sometimes I feel so helpless
    When I remember how the soldiers mocked and
      beat on Him.
A crown of thorns they made, a cruel cross.
    Oh, how much the Saviour must have suffered
      there for you and me.

Sometimes I feel like cryin'
    When I remember how He struggled up the
      Calvary road
And fell beneath the load He bore alone.
    Oh, He walked that awful road that I might
      walk on streets of gold.

Sometimes I feel like cryin'
    When I remember all the agony of Calvary,
And know it was for me that Jesus died.
    Oh, how deeply Jesus must have loved
To give His life for me.

Sometimes I feel like shoutin'
  When I remember Jesus rose again triumphantly.
Oh, what a victory o'er sin and death.
  Oh, because He lives, I, too, shall live
For all eternity.

Sometimes I feel like shoutin'
  When I remember Jesus' promise to return some
    day
To take His children home. Oh, what a day!
  Oh, how can I help but sing when I remember
    all He's done?

A Cross for a Crown

Down from His heavenly throne in the sky,
Out of His ivory palace on high;
Passed from the streets that are paved with pure
  gold,
Through gates of splendor and riches untold.

Born as a babe in a rude manger bed,
Owning no place for to pillow His head;
Walked stony streets, bruised and beaten was He,
Out through the gates and up dark Calvary.

Gave up His life for the sins of all men,
Crucified, buried, He rose up again;
Finished His task, then ascended on high,
Reigns now again from His throne in the sky.

Through gates of splendor He willingly came,
Leaving His throne for a cross of shame;
Rising, triumphant, ascended is He,
Now He's preparing a mansion for me.

Look to the Hills

Lift up your eyes and look on the hills!
Hills where the Master has trod;
Hills where angelic ambassadors came,
Hillsides where man has met God.

Look to the hills near to Bethlehem's inn,
Hills where the angels came down;
Bringing to shepherds the news of His birth,
Yonder in God's chosen town.
Oh, what a place that glorious night!
Flooded with light all around!
Infinite glory here touching the earth;
Sanctified, holy the ground.

Look to the hill near Jerusalem's gate;
See where the Saviour has trod,
Bearing His cross up a hillside of shame,
He, the Beloved of God.
Then on the crest of the hill that He made,
Leaving His glory behind;
God in the flesh here on Calvary's hill,
Died for the sin of mankind.

Look to the hill near where Bethany stands,
Here He ascended that day.
Angelic messengers left us His word,
He would return there some day.
Now we await His return once again,
Not as He came at His birth;
He will return to be King over all,
Reigning supreme on the earth.

Lift up your eyes and look on the hills!
Hills where the Master has trod.
Infinite love sending help from above,
Hillsides where man has met God.

Calvary

Mary's Thoughts at the Cross

"My Son, my Son, why hang you there
     Upon that cruel tree?
For you have done no wrong I know,
     Then why this agony?
Why should I ask? I know full well.
     You are the Christ indeed,
The Son of God come down in flesh
     To save us in our need.

"I thank you, Son, for letting me
     Be part of that great plan
To bring salvation to the earth,
     To rescue fallen man."
Then Mary thought of years gone by—
     When first the angel came
And told her this was God's own Son,
     And Jesus was His name.

And though misunderstood by some,
     She knew within her heart
A miracle from God had come,
     And she would have a part.
And then she thought of Bethlehem—
     The stable and the stall,
The manger bed where shepherds came
     And on their knees did fall.

They told her how the light came down
    And an angel brought the word,
Proclaiming God had sent to earth
    A Saviour, Christ the Lord!
Then later on the Wise Men came
    And precious gifts did bring,
Of gold and frankincense and myrrh,
    To worship this new King.

She thought of all the years she'd watched
    This child become a man,
Until at Cana's marriage feast
    His ministry began.
Those precious, private years were gone.
    Her mother heart must share
Her God-born Son with all the world;
    His work He must declare.

He healed the sick and raised the dead;
    He made the blind to see
And proved by words and deeds of love
    That God's own Son was He.
Through tear-filled eyes she watched Him there,
    While thinking of the past;
His earthly life was nearly gone,
    His work complete at last!

Yet in her grief her heart was full,
    For she had been the one
Whom God the Father chose to be
    The mother of His Son.

How Can It Be?

With tear-filled eyes I stand and gaze
    In almost disbelief
That God's own Son would come to earth
    To bear such pain and grief.

To think that He who made the worlds
    And flung them into space
Would come to earth in human flesh
    And die in such disgrace.

All this I cannot comprehend;
    It is a mystery.
Not knowing why, by faith I cry,
    "Thank God, it was for me."

How can it be? How can it be
    That on a cross at Calvary
The Son of God would come and die
    To save a sinner such as I?

The Greatness of Calvary

The greatest love in all the world
Was shown at Calvary,
When Jesus paid the price of sin
To set the captive free.

The greatest need in all the world
Was met at Calvary,
When God sent down to sinful man
Salvation full and free.

The greatest gift in all the world
Was made at Calvary,
When God the Father gave His Son
To die upon the tree.

The greatest sinner in the world
Can look to Calvary
And find salvation from his sin,
Whoever he may be.

The greatest loss in all the world
May come at Calvary
To those who spurn His saving grace
And die eternally.

The greatest life in all the world
Can start at Calvary,
For those believing in His Son
Shall live eternally.

He Stayed on the Cross

They nailed the hands of Jesus to the cross
 And pierced His feet to hold Him to the tree.
My heart cries out, "Why would the Son of God
   stay hanging there
  And die disgraced in pain and agony?"
The soldiers scoffed, "Come down
  if You're the Christ.
 If You be God, then prove Your word is true."
Though tempted thus, He stayed upon that cruel
   cross and prayed,
 "Forgive them, Lord, they know not
  what they do."

It was His love for you and me, and not the nails,
 That held the Saviour on that awful, cruel tree.
It was His love, and not the nails, that kept Him
   there. Though challenged, too,
  by jeering crowds,
 He stayed and won the victory!
He stayed and conquered death and hell for you
  and me on Calvary!

Invitation

No Need to Be Lonely

No need to be lonely, discouraged and blue;
Don't give up trying, whatever you do.
There's Someone can help you and show you the
way
And bring back the sunshine when skies have
turned gray.

When troubles o'erwhelm you and days seem like
years,
When things seem hopeless, your eyes fill with
tears,
Then go to your Bible, and there you will find
Someone who can cheer you and bring peace of
mind.

That Someone is Jesus; your friend He will be.
Let me introduce you, and then you will see—
He'll walk beside you to cheer and guide you.
There's no one can help you like Jesus, my Lord.

If you do not know Him, why longer delay?
For He is waiting to meet you today.
Your sin He will pardon, He'll live in your heart
To cheer and to guide you. He'll never depart!

A new life He'll give you, your friend He will be;
New joy He will bring you, and then you will see—
He'll walk beside you, to cheer and guide you.
There's no one can help you like Jesus, my Lord.

Come, He Waits for You

Come to the Saviour, He waits for you;
  Come with your heartache and care.
Jesus will give you His wonderful peace,
  Free you from guilt and despair.

Come to the Saviour, He died for you,
  Paid the full price for your sin;
Now He is waiting to save you, my friend,
  Cleanse you without and within.

Come to the Saviour, He rose for you,
  Conquering death and the grave;
Jesus is waiting triumphantly, now,
  Ready and mighty to save.

Come to the Saviour, He waits for you.
  Come without further delay.
Jesus is waiting with arms open wide,
  Come to Him now while you may.

This Is Your Hour

Life has its hours of decision,
Times when a choice must be made;
Now you must make such a judgment,
Whether or not to be saved.

Christ freely offers salvation,
You have the gospel been shown;
Now you must make your decision,
Now you must make your choice known.

You cannot wait 'til tomorrow,
You must this hour make a choice;
God by His Spirit is speaking,
Heed now that small inner voice.

Life has its hours of decision.
Hours when forever you choose
What will determine your future,
You must say yes or refuse.

This is your hour, your hour of decision;
Now you have heard the Good News.
You may accept Him, or you may reject Him;
But now is the time you must choose.

Now

Now is the day of salvation,
Someday you cannot be saved;
Hasten to make your decision,
Let not your choice be delayed.

This is your hour to receive Him,
Now is the time to believe;
Heed now His blest invitation,
Trust—and salvation receive.

Now you must answer the question,
Shall I accept Him today?
Now you must give Him your answer.
Why should you further delay?

Now is the time to receive Him,
Trusting His mercy today;
You may not have a tomorrow,
Turn to Him now while you may.

Now Jesus stands at your heart's door;
Now he would like to come in.
Now will you ask Him to enter,
Cleanse you and save you from sin?

Thankfulness

Thank You for Friends

Thank you, Father, for the priceless gift of a
     friend—
Someone who sees me as I am, but still loves me,
Someone in whom I can confide when things are
     hard
Or share my inner joys, which others may not see
Or understand that they are almost sacred things,
Which, if they fell on ears or hearts that did not
     care,
Might squelch my spirit to the point of deep
     despair.
So thank you, Father, for this cherished gift of
     friends.
And help me, Lord, that if by chance You choose
     to send
Someone to share his inner hurts and joys with me,
I may earn the trust so he can call me "friend."

Thanksgiving Is Thanksliving

Thanksgiving is thanksliving,
Not just some empty talk.
The best way to say thank you
Is by the way you walk.

Thanksgiving is thanksliving.
One deed is worth much more
Than countless good intentions
Or wishes by the score.

Thanksgiving is thanksliving.
The way the world will know
Our gratitude to Jesus
Is by the life we show.

How Should I Say Thank You?

Say thank you to Jesus for what He has done
By doing whatever you can.
The deed may be small and be hidden from
      view
And may go unnoticed by men.

Remember the lad with the fishes and loaves;
He gave all he had though it seemed very small.
Wherever you are, whatever you have,
Say thank you by doing and giving your all.

Say thank you to Jesus in all that you do,
For this is the gospel according to you.
The words that you say may not mean much, my
      friend,
Unless they are proved by the things that you do.

Remember to Say Thank You

My little girl went out the door;
I hugged and squeezed her just once more,
Reminding her as oft before,
"Remember to say thank you."

And then the thought occurred to me,
I'd better check again to see
How long since I on bended knee
Remembered to say thank you.

Thanksgiving and Praise

Let us praise the Lord together with thanksgiving
For the blessings we have known,
For the mercy He has shown.
Let us praise the Lord together with thanksgiving.

Let us thank the Lord for Jesus and salvation,
For His death on Calvary
From our sin to set us free.
Let us thank the Lord for Jesus and salvation.

Let us thank the Lord for daily bread and shelter,
For His faithful loving care,
For the home He will prepare.
Let us thank the Lord for daily bread and shelter.

Let us worship God in prayerful adoration.
Praise and honor now we bring
As we crown Him Lord and King.
Let us worship God in prayerful adoration.

Let us shout and sing a mighty "Hallelujah"!
Grateful voices now we raise
In a sacrifice of praise.
Let us shout and sing a mighty "Hallelujah"!

For All He Has Done

Be thankful to God for all He has done,
To save us from sin by sending us His Son;
Be grateful He gave us the gift of His Word,
Redemption in writing, revealing Christ the Lord.

Be grateful for those whose blood, sweat and tears,
Brought us the Good News mid anger, scorn and
      jeers;
Thank God they were faithful in sharing the Word,
Or we would be lost, having never ever heard.

The debt that we owe, we ne'er can repay,
But we can respond by going forth today
And taking the gospel to those who are lost,
Like others before us who counted not the cost.

We love you, O God, for all You have done,
Declaring your Word and sending us Your Son;
Now grant us the courage, the wisdom, the grace,
To make known the gospel to ev'ry land and race.

In Everything Give Thanks

In everything give thanks,
  Fear not the raging storm;
    God moves in a mysterious way
His wonders to perform.

In everything give thanks,
  Whatever be the test;
    For in God's providence,
He sends us what is best.

In everything give thanks;
  God watches day and night,
    Protecting, caring for His own;
Their good is His delight.

In everything give thanks,
God lives and reigns supreme
 And now prepares a home for us
Beyond our fondest dream.

 In everything give thanks;
In gratitude to Him
 Lift up your voice! Give thanks! Rejoice!
In everything give thanks.

Give Thanks

Give thanks to God for everything—
 The sunshine and the rain,
The joy and grief, the gain and loss,
 The pleasure and the pain.

For every good and perfect gift
 Give thanks to God above;
He daily showers blessings down
 In mercy, grace and love.

Give thanks when difficulties rise,
 For God is ever near;
His purposes are for your good;
 Someday He'll make them clear.

Give thanks, although your present test
 Is difficult to bear;
A crown eternal may be yours
 Forevermore to wear.

Give thanks to God, for He still reigns
    And watches o'er His own;
He guards His children night and day,
    Perhaps to them unknown.

We Thank Thee for Thy Word

We thank Thee for Thy Word, O God,
    Upon this rock we stand;
Its truth and wisdom shall not fail,
    All else is sinking sand.

We seek Thee in Thy Holy Word.
    O help us, Lord, to see
Thy greatness, power, love and might,
    Thy grace and majesty.

Lord, speak from Thy eternal Word,
    Reveal Thyself, we pray;
And from its pages give us light,
    To guide us on our way.

O gentle Holy Spirit, come,
    Reveal Thy truth, we pray;
That from its precepts we may learn
    To walk with Thee each day.

The Birth of Christ

The Miracle of Christmas

Many were the miracles
The night of Jesus' birth;
The wonders in the eastern sky,
The signs upon the earth.
Mary was a miracle
By prophets long foretold;
A virgin bringing forth a Son,
Amazing to behold!
But the miracle of miracles,
The wonder of it all,
Was not the virgin Mary,
The stable and the stall;
It was that God Himself had come,
Incarnate as a child,
That God and sinful man might be
Forever reconciled.

Angels from the realms on high
To lowly shepherds came,
Proclaiming peace, goodwill to men
And glory to His name.
Wise Men saw the star appear,
Announcing Christ the King;
To guide them on their journey west,
Their precious gifts to bring.
But the miracle of miracles
Was not the eastern star,
The angels near to Bethlehem,
Or Wise Men from afar;
It was that God Himself had come,
Incarnate as a child,
That God and sinful man might be
Forever reconciled.

The Keeper of the Inn

Long years ago in Bethlehem
    The keeper of the inn,
For Joseph, Mary and the Babe,
    Would make no room within.
He bolted fast the wooden door
    And made them go away
Into a bedless stable, where
    They slept upon the hay.
Now you are keeper of the inn,
    And Jesus stands outside;
The latchstring hangs inside the door.
    Will you let Him inside?

Once Jesus came in human flesh
    To die for all our sin.
Now He in Spirit comes to man,
    And asks to enter in.
Now you are keeper of the inn,
    The inn which is your heart.
The choice is yours to ask Him in
    Or bid Him to depart.
O Jesus, come in human flesh
    To save us from our sin,
I gladly open wide the door;
    Come now and enter in.

The World Knew Him Not

The world knew Him not, and they left Him no
    room,
    This Child whom the prophets foretold.
The world He created had left Him no place
    But a manger bed, rugged and cold.
The star in the heavens announced Jesus' birth,
    The angels sang praises that night;
Still the world did not see that the Saviour had
    come
    To turn men from darkness to light.

If Jesus would come to the inn of your heart
    And ask for a place there today,
Would you recognize Him as God's only Son
    And bid Him to enter and stay?
His Word, not a star, is the light that we see;
    Redeemed ones, not angels, sing praise.
Let all who receive Him as Saviour draw near
    And join in the song that we raise!

The Star of Bethlehem

In Bethlehem's sky rose a bright, shining star
   That guided the Wise Men who came from afar.
They followed its light as their gifts they did bring
   To give this young child, who would someday
     be King.
The Light they were seeking was brighter by far
   Than that which was shining from Bethlehem's
     star,
For it would shine on through the ages to come.
   Its Light was eternal; this child was God's Son.

This Light which from Bethlehem's manger began
   Would someday shine out to reveal unto man,
That He who began in so lowly a place
   Had brought us salvation with mercy and grace.
The world lay in sin like the darkness of night,
   But Jesus came forth with redemption and light,
That all who would seek Him, like Wise Men of old,
   Will find Him more precious than incense and
     gold.

Love Song

I looked to find a love song
That anyone could sing,
With words of deep devotion,
That strength and joy would bring,
A love song warm and tender,
A story pure and true,
So all would know its meaning,
Not just a special few.

God wrote that love song
Many years ago
In Bethlehem Judaea
So all the world would know
That in His Son, called Jesus
By angels from above,
The world could see more clearly
How perfect is His love.

This love song tells of Jesus,
The stable and the hay,
The shepherds and the Wise Men
Who came to kneel and pray.
But then this blessed story
Goes on to Calvary,
Where Jesus gave His life-blood
So all His love could see.

The Resurrection

God Is Not Dead

Though some may say that God is dead,
I know this cannot be:
I'll tell you why I know He lives,
'Tis there for all to see.

I look into the Word of God,
His presence there to see;
And day by day in many ways,
He shows Himself to me.
I look into the sky above,
His glory there I trace;
The handiwork of God I see
Revealed in outer space.

I look behind at years gone by,
The hand of God to see;
A tender, loving, all-wise God
Has made a way for me.
I look at men with lives transformed,
These slaves of sin set free;
And know this living miracle
The work of God to be.

God is not dead, I know He lives today;
God is not dead, I meet Him when I pray.
I sense His presence with me night and day;
Within my heart I know that God is not dead.

Each Day

I watched him playing in his crib,
This tiny little lad,
And thought of all the years ahead
For me to be his dad.

So soon I watched him as he went
Inside the grade school door.
The first few years had quickly passed,
But there would be lots more.

I watched him walk across the stage,
And high school days were done.
I hardly could believe my eyes—
That this man was my son.

So much of life is still ahead;
In fact, it's just begun.
But now I realize anew
How fast the race is run.

So as the years go rushing by,
I'll try to make each day
To count for something that's worthwhile
Before it slips away.

This is the day the Lord hath made;
Rejoice then, and be glad,
And never cease to thank the Lord
For those two words: "Hi, Dad."

Scenes of Yesterday

I wandered through the hallways of my mind
And looked into the rooms of memory.
I saw the many scenes of yesterday
And wondered how they shaped my destiny.
Some rooms were filled with laughter and with
      mirth,
The colors bright, and music filled the air.
Some rooms were dark, but straining, I could see
The tearful faces, filled with deep despair.
And then the Landlord came and bid me stay
And dwell within the rooms that I should choose.
The future days depend upon my choice
Of rooms, now waiting there for me to use.
Why should I linger in the darkened rooms?
Enough of them! They had their day, and so
I'll dwell within the joy-filled memories
That give my light of life an added glow.

Music Is a Temple

My music is a temple;
Within its walls I find
A place to meet with God Himself
And leave the world behind.

The structure of this temple,
Instead of wood and stone,
Is made of melody and song,
Of timbre and of tone.

With instruments and voices,
With hymns and songs I raise
My inner soul to God in prayer,
In worship and in praise.

With joyful heart I enter
And join the happy throng
Who sing and praise and bless His Name
From hearts that burst with song.

When rest of soul I'm seeking,
In quiet song I find
The Prince of Peace will meet me there,
And grant me peace of mind.

When words of praise escape me,
I often find a hymn
Expressing all the things I feel
But cannot say to Him.

Sometimes when I am lonely,
New comfort I can take
From one who proved long before
That God does not forsake.

Disheartened by some trial,
New courage I can find
To hear the truth some singing saint
Hath left for all mankind.

An organ softly playing
Brings sweet communion here,
Like incense rising up to Him,
A heartfelt, wordless prayer.

This temple built of mine,
By God Himself designed,
Has room for all to enter in
And leave the world behind.

At This Altar

A Wedding Prayer

Lord, we kneel before this altar,
Here to pledge this sacred vow;
By Thy holy presence seal it,
With Thy blessing it endow.

Here we pledge to one another
All the love our hearts possess;
Make this flesh as one before Thee,
This our pledge we here express.

Make this love which Thou hast given,
Love which only came from Thee,
Full and deep and pure and lasting;
Make it like Thine own to be.

Holy Spirit, in this union
All Thy precious fruit instill;
Make our lives to be of service;
Spend them on Thy perfect will.

It Seemed So Small

It seemed so small, that little spark,
But soon a giant flame
Was spreading far beyond control,
Destroying trees and game.

It seemed so small, that hasty word,
That crossed my lips that day,
But soon it spread like forest fire,
Much to my great dismay!

It seemed so small, that little prayer,
When I was all alone,
But wondrous things took place because
God heard it from His throne.

A Prayer

Speak from Thy Word in this quiet hour.
Teach me to live by Thy Spirit's pow'r.
Open my heart so that I may see
More of Thyself and Thy purpose in me.

The Teenager's Friend

Jesus was a teenage boy;
    He fully understands
The problems that I face each day,
    My feelings and my plans.
So when a crisis faces me
    And questions come each day,
I seek His guidance, for I know
    He, too, has passed this way.

Jesus was a teenage boy,
    But more than that, I know,
He was the Son of God Himself;
    The Bible tells us so.
Because He was both God and man,
    I've found He understands
And has the power to supply
    Whatever life demands.

Bless This Woman

Bless this woman, Lord, we pray!
Guide her footsteps night and day.
Grant her courage, joy and peace.
Let Thy blessings never cease.
Thank you, Lord, that through the years,
In the midst of toil and tears,
Thou hast kept her strong and true,
Seeking out Thy will to do,
Holding forth the Word of Life,
Standing firm in times of strife,
Trusting in Thy mighty hand,
Pressing on at Thy command.

Thank you, Lord, that through her days
Thou hast filled her heart with praise.
Thou hast kept her faithfully
Pointing other souls to Thee,
Helping others in their need
By a kindly word or deed,
Sharing every anxious care,
Giving of herself in prayer.
Bless this woman, Lord, we plead!
In the past Thou hast indeed!
Make her future life to be
Like incense rising up to Thee.

Bless This Man

Bless this man, O Lord, we pray!
Guide his footsteps night and day.
Grant him courage, joy and peace.
Let Thy blessings never cease.
Thank you, Lord, that through the years,
In the midst of toil and tears,
Thou hast kept him strong and true,
Seeking out Thy will to do,
Holding forth the Word of Life,
Standing firm in times of strife,
Trusting in Thy mighty hand,
Pressing on at Thy command.

Thank you, Lord, that through his days
Thou hast filled his heart with praise.
Thou hast kept him faithfully
Pointing other men to Thee,
Helping others in their need
By a kindly word or deed,
Sharing every anxious care,
Giving of himself in prayer.
Bless this man, O Lord, we plead!
In the past Thou hast indeed!
Make his future life to be
Like incense rising up to Thee.

Copyrights

144

145

146

148

Topical Index

154

155